SCHOOL RHYMES

SCHOOL RHYMES

Volume One

Poems and illustrations by
KATHY HARRISON

GSP

School Rhymes: Volume One
Kathy Harrison

Published by Greyhound Self-Publishing 2013
Malvern, Worcestershire, United Kingdom.

Printed and bound by Aspect Design
89 Newtown Road, Malvern, Worcs. WR14 1PD
United Kingdom
Tel: 01684 561567
E-mail: allan@aspect-design.net
Website: www.aspect-design.net

A copy of this book has been deposited with the
British Library Board.

ISBN 978-1-909219-09-0

CONTENTS

PREFACE

My daughter, Kathy, was a very capable young woman, full of fun but also a quiet observer of people and situations, and always there for anyone needing support or encouragement.

She died in 1994, leaving her poems to her college friend, Joanne, who, eighteen years later, typed out the children's poems as a Christmas present for Kathy's little grandchildren. She also sent me a copy, and I decided to explore the possibility of getting it published. Aspect Design were very helpful and patient and the result was the delightful little book of *Creepy Crawlies.*

There were, it transpired, rather more poems in that box, complete with illustrations, so Joanne and her husband, Martin, kindly made me copies of them all, hence this book, with two more to come. My special thanks, therefore, to Joanne and Martin, to Jane for her computer skills, and to Allan and his staff at Aspect Design.

Kathy's Mum.

MORNINGS

'Have I got to go to school today?' I ask my mum each day,
And when the answer's 'Yes, you do', I really make her pay.

I tell her that it's boring,
That I haven't any friends.
I tell her all I do is cry
Until the school day ends.
I say I've got a headache
And I'm starting to feel sick.
I say I want to stay at home.
I try out every trick.
I walk to school so slowly,
Clinging to her hand.
I tell her that she's horrible,
And that she doesn't understand.
When I'm feeling really awkward
I can even start to cry.
Then mum looks really worried
As she's waving me goodbye.

I wait until she's out of sight, put a big smile on my face,
Then stroll into the classroom. Yes, I really love this place.

GIFTS FOR THE TEACHER

I like to bring my teacher
A little gift each day
My mother tries to stop me,
'But she longs for them', I say.

Sometimes its a daisy,
Sometimes it's a rose,
Once it was a dandelion
I waved under her nose.

Another time I brought a conker,
And once it was a petal.
Once I made a big mistake
And picked a stinging nettle.

Some days I draw her pictures
That I tell her she can keep.
Johnny Roberts in my class
Says I am a creep.

I don't care what the others say,
I don't even want to hear.
My teacher always smiles and says,
'That's really lovely, dear'.

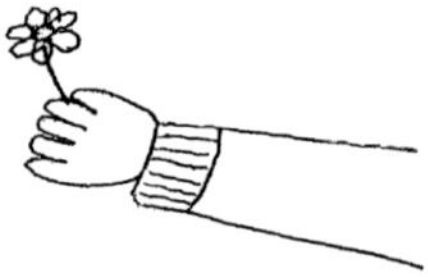

STAGE FRIGHT

In our class assembly
I've got to stand and say,
'Good morning, everybody,'
In a most appealing way.

I've been trying very hard
To make it loud and clear
So that all the people
In the hall will hear.

The day has come at last,
And I stand up tall and say,
'Good evening, anybody,'
In a most appalling way.

TEACHER'S LEGS

I love to stroke my teacher's legs
When I'm sitting at her feet.
First she shuffles, then she kicks
And wriggles in her seat.

She turns and says, 'I'm not a cat,
So you're not allowed to touch.'
She shouldn't let them dangle there
If she doesn't like it much!

PIANO PLAYING?

We have to have hymn practice
First thing on Friday.
I'm sure we'd all sing better
If Miss Matthews didn't play.

She plays the piano dreadfully,
I think she's worse than me.
While she's trying to find the right notes
We just wait patiently.

She plays so slowly, we forget
What we began to sing.
I think I could do better
With one arm in a sling!

Though sometimes she hits a right note,
Nine out of ten are wrong.
Sometimes, if we're lucky,
We recognise the song.

Once we actually finished a hymn
Almost all together.
Someone should find the piano key
And lock it up forever!

LAST ON THE REGISTER

Why am I last on the register and at the end of every list?
Whichever class I'm in it is the same.
All I want is to be first for once, or even in the middle.
I think it must have something to do with my last name.
Do you want to know what my name is, then?
It's only
Samantha Abigail Zen.

NEW BOY

I like to think I'm cocky
I like to think I'm brave
I like to think I'm real grown-up and cool.
In fact I'm rather lonely,
I'm timid and I'm shy.
It's scary when you're a new boy at the school.

TEACHERS DON'T KNOW EVERYTHING

I really thought my teacher knew all there was to know . . .

She knows every single number
She knows how sunflowers grow.
She knows how to do up shoelaces
And how to tie my bow.
She knows all about the piano
Which notes are high or low.
She knows how to paint and colour
And how to knit and sew.
She knows all about the weather
And why the cold winds blow.
She knows about the rain and sun
Why sometimes we get snow.
She knows why spiders run so fast
Why snails are very slow.
She even knows the difference
Between a blackbird and a crow.
She knows each part of the body
From head down to the toe.
When we go outside the classroom
She knows which way to go.

I really thought my teacher knew all there was to know.
I was really disappointed to find this wasn't so.
I discovered there was one thing that she really didn't know.
She didn't even have a clue that my hamster's name was 'Flo'!

WHERE DO THOSE TEACHERS SLEEP?

When I'm sitting in assembly, bored out of my mind,
I always take a good look round.
There's something I must find.

I look up at the ceiling, I look all round the floor,
And when I wander through the school
I check through every door.

I've looked all round the playground,
In every cupboard too.
I've checked the courtyard and the shed
But I have not found a clue.

One night I'm going to leave my house
And very quietly creep
Into the school to find out
Where those teachers sleep!

SUPPLY TEACHER

Sometimes our teacher isn't there,
She's on a course or ill in bed.
Then in comes a supply teacher
Followed by the head.

The head mistress says something like,
'Now I want every one of you
To show how considerate you are
And how much work you do.'

We wait for the head to leave the class,
We watch her disappear,
Then we do all the things we wouldn't do
If our own teacher was here.

We chatter while she's talking,
We play our silly games.
Once, when she did the register
We answered the wrong names.

We all do as little as possible,
Pretend that it's too hard.
We usually end up colouring,
Or making Miss a card.

We enjoy these days the teacher's off,
We have a laugh and lots of fun,
But when she returns, and it's back to work
It's a relief for everyone.

MISS

'Teacher, can you help me?'
'Miss, can we play this game?'
We always get the same response,
'Please use my proper name.'
But since Miss Higginbottom came
Things haven't been the same.
'Miss' or 'Teach' or 'Teacher'
She prefers to her real name!

SWINGING

I do love swinging on my chair,
Balancing on two legs.
I've only ever fallen backwards twice.
One day no doubt I'll hurt myself –
My teacher says I will,
But I'm not too good at taking her advice!

THE CARETAKER

Our caretaker's name is Wally,
And that's just what he is.
He really seems to like to have a moan.
He lives alone in the big house
Next door to the junior school,
And I'm not at all surprised he's on his own.

He never says 'Hello' to us,
He never talks – he grunts.
His face is really grumpy all the time.
And little accidents on the floor
Or spillages with paint
He treats as if they were a major crime.

He obviously doesn't like his work,
I've never seen him smile.
In fact, he scares me right out of my wits.
One day I'd like to spite him
And throw up on the floor,
Then laugh at him while he's cleaning up the bits!

TOILETS

At school I hate the toilets
They nearly always smell,
And even from a distance
They make me feel unwell.

The seats are always soaking wet,
There's puddles on the floor,
There's toilet paper everywhere,
And I can never lock the door.

I always have to hold my breath
When I go and wash my hands.
I've seen my teacher do it too,
So I know she understands.

I don't drink anything all day,
So I don't have to go.
I sometimes have to cross my legs
Or hop from toe to toe.

My mother's never realised
Exactly what I do,
Although I'm always running home
And dashing to the loo!

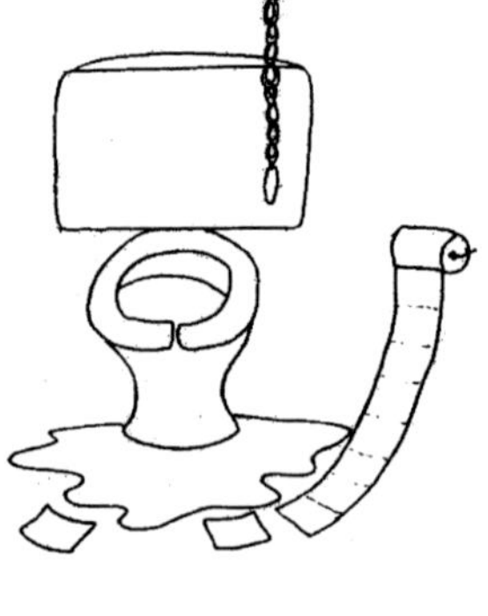

MY LITTLE BROTHER

My little brother's starting
At my school today.
Mum's told me to look after him
When we go out to play.

He's no more than a baby,
He's really very small.
He'll be hopeless in the playground.
He can't even catch a ball.

I don't want to have to play with him.
Mum says I'm not to moan.
I'll only do it this week
And then he's on his own.

My brother is just starting
His second week at school.
He's not as awful as I thought,
In fact, he's rather cool.

He's really good at fighting –
He never used to be.
He's a wizard with the football,
And he runs as fast as me.

My friends and I have always
Played well with one another.
Today I'm playing by myself
They've gone to find my brother.

THE PLAYGROUND

My first time in the playground
I stood and watched in fright,
Cowering in a corner
So I was out of sight.

The thought of all those children
Filled my heart with fear.
I stood there without moving,
Hoping no one would come near.

All the children seemed so big,
And I felt very small.
I was very nearly tempted
To sneak back into school.

There was running,
skipping,
fighting,
kicking.

There was whispering,
screaming,
shouting,
dreaming.

There were scratches,
tears,
laughs
and jeers.

There were lots of big girls,
lots of big boys,
lots of bullies,
lots of noise.

I tried to walk to the other side
To put my rubbish in the bin.
I got knocked over three times,
And someone kicked me on the shin.

I went over to the teacher
And made her hold my hand.
I'll join in when I'm bigger.
I hope you understand.

SCHOOL DINNERS

Mum likes me to have dinners to give me something hot.
She doesn't seem to understand
That usually they're not.

Most of the food is lukewarm by the time I join the queue,
The vegetables are soggy,
And the best food's all gone too.

The chips are never too bad so I have them every day.
I always eat them all up
And chuck the rest away.

I'm meant to chose the healthy foods to make me grow up strong.
Mum says they taste delicious,
But mum is often wrong.

The pudding's not too awful, though the custard's made too thick.
The jelly's always runny,
And the shortbread makes me sick.

I usually have an apple, (well, it's healthy anyway)
And the dinner lady sometimes
Lets me take it out to play.

All in all, the only dish that makes me lick my lips
Is sausage and beans (when they're hot)
And a lovely pile of chips.

READING

I've really gone off reading. I used to be quite good,
Now I'm bored with practising, although I know I should.

Instead of taking my book home I leave it at the school.
When mum questioned me about it I said, 'That's the new rule'.

When my teacher asks me if I've got my reading book
I always tell her that I'll just go and have a look.

After lots of searching I say it can't be found.
She tells me when I get home to have a good look round.

I've hidden it in the sand tray, I've hidden it near the pegs.
My teacher says my reading books must have their own two legs!

But this morning, as I feared, she made me read another book,
She said she wasn't going to let me off the hook.

I read the book so easily I was really quite amazed.
She said I read extremely well. I went off in a daze.

I think perhaps my reading book will reappear somehow!
I think I'll take it home tonight
Because I *do* like reading now.

WET PLAYS

The last few days its been raining –
It means we can't get out.
I really need to let off steam,
To run and scream and shout.

When playtime comes we eat our crisps
Sitting on a chair.
When we've finished you just wouldn't believe,
The mess that's everywhere.

The windows get all steamed up,
The classroom starts to smell,
There's dripping raincoats on the pegs,
Mud on the floor as well.

Out comes the class's 'Wet Play Box'
Which is really, really boring.
There's colouring books which are all full up,
Paper and crayons for drawing.

There's some books which I've already read
With half the pages torn out,
Most of the comics have been ripped,
And the felt pens have run out.

And then, before the bell goes,
We have to tidy up the mess –
Crumbs and paper everywhere.
Yes, dry days are the best.

And because we cannot go outside
To shout and run about,
We're really noisy all day long,
Which makes our teacher shout.

I really hate wet days at school,
It really is a pain.
I think we ought to stay at home
When the weather forecast is rain!

GETTING CHANGED FOR PE

I don't mind doing PE
But I don't like getting changed.
I don't mind doing it at home
But at school it just feels strange.

There's so many buttons, zips and bows
And fasteners to do up,
And I'm always last to finish,
Which makes me feel fed up.

We always have to hurry,
My teacher makes us rush.
If I spend too long on anything
She tells me not to fuss.

I always lose a sock or shoe,
It takes hours to track it down.
I usually find it in someone's bag
Or hidden on the ground.

And it always seems to be me
And never all the rest
Who, just as I've finished dressing,
Finds a forgotten vest!

PENCILS

I like my pencil really sharp
So it's pointed like a pin.
It's great to use as a weapon
Or for poking holes in things.

If you find a gap between the tables
And put some paper on it
You can make some really perfect holes
By pushing your pencil through it.

I go up to the rubbish bin
When my teacher isn't near.
I sharpen my pencil over again
Till at last it disappears.

I tell my teacher that it's gone.
He questions everyone.
Sometimes, if I'm lucky
I get a brand new pointed one!

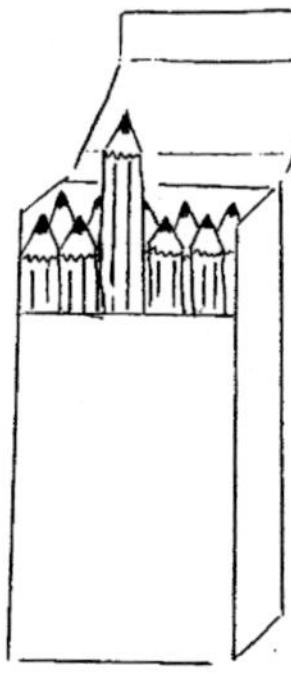

COPYCAT

I think I'll copy Dionne,
She always gets things right.
Dionne's writing's clear and neat
And she's very, very bright.

I don't know what I'm copying,
It's hard work, but it's fun.
I hope my teacher's pleased with me
And can tell me what I've done.

MUSIC AND MOVEMENT

I cannot start to understand
Why I've got to be a tree.
I'm waving my branches in the breeze,
Rustling and shaking all my leaves.
Can somebody, somewhere, tell me please
Why can't I just be me?

CHRISTMAS PARTY

At Christmas we have a party,
We all bring in some food.
It's the best day of the year,
That's what I think.
There's sausages and sandwiches,
Piles of crisps and cakes,
Chocolate biscuits, ice cream
And lots of squash to drink.

We play party games
And sing some songs,
We dance until we drop
Then we eat our party food up
Much too quick.
Father Christmas comes
And gives presents to us all,
Then it's time to say goodbye.
It was all great fun,
But, boy, do I feel sick!

HAIR

When I'm listening to a story
And trying to concentrate
Or when I'm sitting in assembly
There's one thing that I hate.
Someone starts playing with my hair,
It's always mine – it isn't fair.

They fiddle with it,
Twiddle it,
Stroke it,
Poke it,
Pull it,
Plait it,
Fluff it,
Flatten it.

I can't turn round and say a thing
When talking's not allowed.
I can't get up and move away
Or squeal and scream out loud.
When I get home I really shout
When I have to brush the knots all out.

I've tried to sit all by myself
Or where nobody can find me,
But somehow someone manages
To creep secretly behind me.
Even with my back against the chair
They still succeed in getting to my hair.

I've asked my mum to cut it
And make it really short.
She said it took so long to grow
She'll do nothing of the sort.
Perhaps I'll have to wear a hat,
But I bet they'd even get under that.

I decided to retaliate
In story time today.
I attacked the girl in front of me,
I soon was well away.
I stroked and twirled and twisted,
I tried to make a bun,
I discovered that this pastime
Was really rather fun!

So now I've never got a clue
what story's being read.
I'm far too busy concentrating
On some poor person's head.

As long as it's not happening to you,
I recommend it – I really do!

INTEREST TABLES

On our interest table
We've got a wormery.
I could sit and watch it all day long,
Those worms really fascinate me.

Our interest table's really great,
We've got all sorts of things,
Lots of creepy crawlies
And even things with wings.

We've got a hairy caterpillar,
A spider and two slugs.
There's a jar of slimy snails,
And some other nasty bugs.

There's books to look at,
Signs to read,
A gerbil that we
Have to feed.

There's magnifying glasses
To study all these creatures.
It's the most interesting table in the room,
Except, of course, for the teachers!

THE MYSTERY OF THE DIRTY MARKS

First I take my jumper off, then roll up my sleeves,
Then I chose a painting apron that reaches to my knees.

Then I pick a trusted friend to fasten both the flaps,
One more last inspection to check for any gaps.

Then I have a great time with paint or glue or clay,
And if I had the option I'd carry on all day.

But all too soon I have to stop. I head out to the sink
And scrub my hands and fingernails till they're really clean and pink.

What happens after that is an unsolved mystery,
I've tried to tell my mother but she just won't listen to me.

As soon as I get home from school I rush upstairs to change
And then I always notice something very strange.

There's always paint or glue or clay somewhere on my clothes.
How on earth it got there heaven only knows!

THE FLICKER

David Brown flicks pencils
And crayons across the class.
You never see them leave his hand,
Just hear them whizzing past.

'Who's flicking pencils?' asks the teacher.
No-one says a word.
David just keeps on working
As if he hadn't heard.

One day he flicked a crayon at me
When I was sitting in my place.
I picked it up and flicked it back.
It hit him in the face.

Of course the teacher saw me,
My knees began to shake,
He shouted at me fiercely
And made me miss my break.

David started laughing.
There was nothing I could do.
O David Brown, please tell me
Why he never catches you!

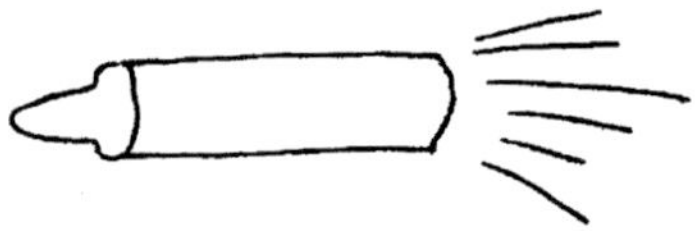

TRACY JONES

Tracy Jones in our class is really quiet and timid,
She'll answer her name on the register, but that's about her limit.

It's really quite extraordinary how she never makes a noise,
But I heard her shouting at her mum so I know she's got a voice.

She won't talk to the teacher, she'll never talk to me,
We tried to help her join in, now we just let her be.

One day a strange thing happened. On a sunny afternoon
We were practising for sports day which was taking place quite soon.

We were practising our races, and while we watched and cheered
Tracy Jones was joining in – I couldn't believe my ears.

She was jumping up and down, screaming and shouting names
Of children that she wanted to win the races and the games.

We never had a moment's peace after that momentous day,
She was making up for lost time and she had so much to say.

Her voice is really piercing, it really gets to me.
Sometimes I wish she'd just go back to how she used to be.

SCHOOL MEDICALS

I've got to have a medical,
My mother's going to come.
My best friend told me yesterday
That they'll want to see my bum.
He told me there's lots of nurses looking,
It isn't just the one.
I don't known if it's really true
But I don't dare ask my mum.

I'm getting really worried,
I couldn't sleep last night,
But all my mother says is that
It's going to be all right.
I'm thinking of being really brave
And putting up a fight.
I haven't quite decided,
But I think I really might.

It's over now – I've done it,
And it really wasn't bad.
I was in and out in minutes,
And nurse called me a lovely lad.
I shouldn't have listened to my friend,
I really must be mad.
Next time I'll be more sensible,
I'll believe my mum and dad.

MUM'S COMING UP THE SCHOOL TODAY

Mum's coming up the school today to see the work I've done.
I think she's a little worried that I'm having too much fun.

Every day I tell her that what I do all day,
Apart from a bit of reading, is lots and lots of play.

When I come out of the classroom she's always sure to say,
'Come on, darling, tell me what you've done today'.

I say I've done no writing and I've not done any sums,
But I've been playing in the Wendy House along with all my chums.

Strangely, she believes me, never any doubt,
So she thinks she's coming up the school to sort my teacher out.

She's going to get a shock today – it'll be a big surprise
When she sees how many books I've filled.
She won't believe her eyes.

She'll have no reason to complain when she sees the work I've done.
I expect she'll also wonder how I still have so much fun!

FIRE DRILL

The most exciting thing each term
Which gives us all a thrill
Is when the fireman comes along
To give us our fire drill.

We don't know when he's coming,
We don't see him arrive,
No-one tells us anything
So it's always a surprise.

We're sitting working quietly
When the alarm bell starts to ring.
Everyone, even the teacher,
Jumps out of their skin.

Then we all walk very quickly
Without a single sound
To join the other classes
Lining up in the playground.

There's nudges and there's whispers,
'Is there really a fire inside?'
'Has anyone seen smoke or flames?'
'Has anybody died?'

When we've all answered the register
And been told we did quite well,
There's so much to say to one another,
So many stories we have to tell.

We talk of times we've rescued people
From black smoke and from flames.
We tell of great adventures
And make up 'Fireman' games.

Imaginations are working overtime,
Some children say they're burnt,
Others are scared to go inside
In case the flames will hurt.

Teacher has to calm us down.
She talks to everyone.
The thrills are over 'til next term,
Unless we have a *real* one.

LATE!

The school bell rang at bang on three,
I went running out of class,
But mummy wasn't out there
So I sat down on the grass.

I stayed there for five minutes
Playing with a stone.
I watched till everybody else
Had disappeared off home.

Then I went back to my teacher –
That's what we're meant to do.
She told me not to worry,
My mum would turn up soon.

I sharpened all the pencils,
Picked the bits up off the floor,
But all I wanted was for mum
To walk in through the door.

I was taken to the office
And sat down on a chair,
Given a pile of boring books.
No-one seemed to care.

I thought I'd have to stay there
All night on my own.
I was starting to feel hungry.
I just wanted to go home.

Then all at once it dawned on me
She didn't love me any more,
And all because that morning
I'd spilled orange on the floor.

Suddenly mum rushed in the door,
Said she'd just been down the town,
She'd driven to the roundabout,
When the car had broken down.

I hadn't made a fuss till then
But I couldn't stop the tears.
She said she was only ten minutes late.
It had seemed more like ten years!

ME AND MY BEST FRIEND

My best friend doesn't like me,
She called me a fat pig.
I'd like to say the same to her
If she wasn't quite so big.
She says that it is all my fault
Because I went and sat with Lynne.
She wrote me a rude letter
Which I put straight in the bin.

My best friend doesn't like me.
My sister says, 'So what?'
My teacher doesn't seem to care,
But I care quite a lot.
She wouldn't be my partner
When we went out for PE,
So I had to partner Michael,
And the whole class laughed at me.

My best friend doesn't like me,
Though she's just passed me a sweet,
And when we went to lunch today
She did save me a seat.
I'm going round to play with her
When school comes to an end.
We love each other really,
Me and my best friend.

THE SCHOOL PHOTOGRAPHER

We all look forward to the day
when the school photographer comes.
He brings his special camera
And takes pictures for our mums.

The night before he's coming
my mum washes my hair,
A nice clean shirt and school tie
Are laid out on my chair.

He sometimes calls us silly names,
which really make us giggle,
We're falling about laughing,
Then he tells us not to wriggle!

Last time he called me 'Superman'
and my best friend 'Frizzy Head'.
He called Samantha 'Gingernut'
Her face went really red.

He makes us sit up very straight,
hands resting on our knees,
He makes us say all kinds of words
Much sillier than 'cheese'.

By the time we get back to our class
he's really wound us up.
The teacher knows we won't work now
So she usually just gives up.

LETTERS

Sometimes at the end of school
There's letters to give out.
My teacher gives us all one each,
Tells us what they're all about.

She makes us put them in our bags,
Or hold on to them tight.
She sends us out one at a time
When we've all said 'Goodnight'.

She checks we've got our letters
As we walk out of the door,
So how come there's always three at least
Left lying on the floor?